enjoy!

What a great year!

王之渙 – 登鸛雀樓

WANG Zhihuan – Atop the Stork Pavilion Lookout

白日依山盡

黃河入海流

欲窮千里目

更上一層樓

- From the pavilion one sees the sun setting behind the mountains,
- Unrelentingly towards the sea the Yellow River flows;
- In order to see thousands of miles further afield,
- To a higher level one must go.

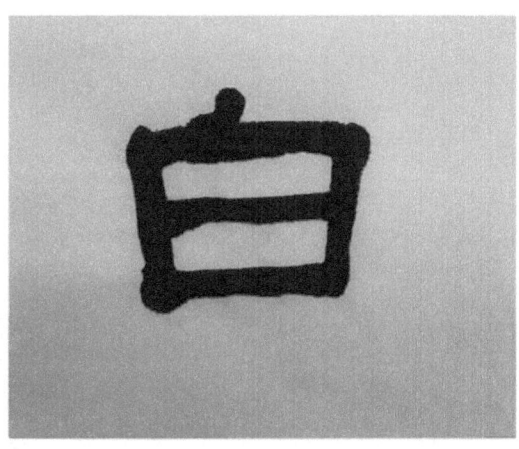

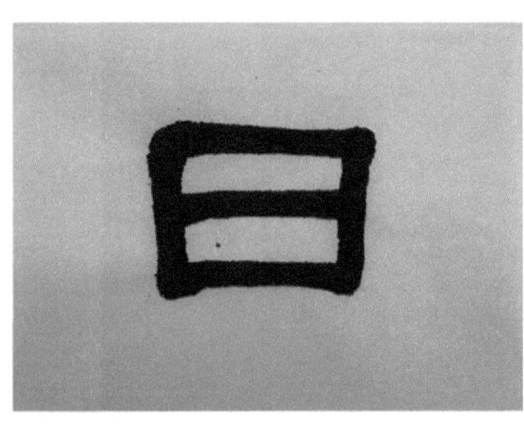

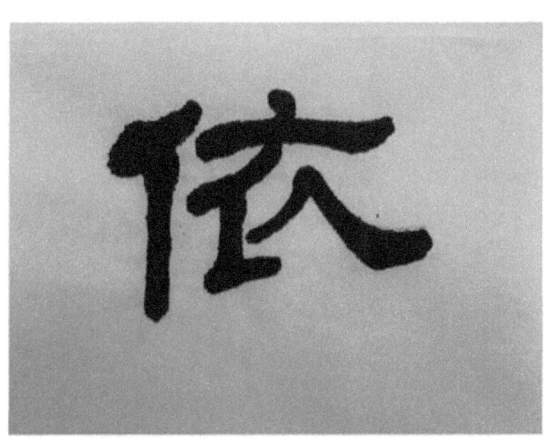

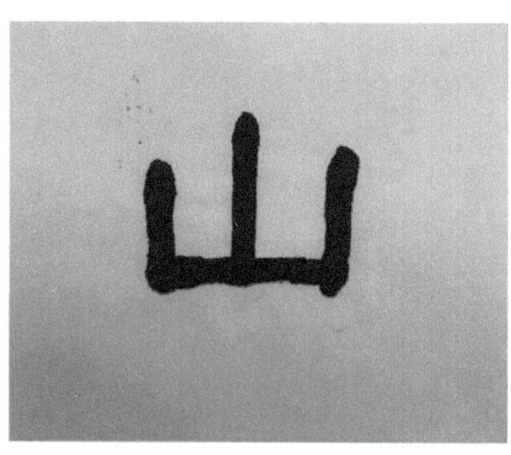

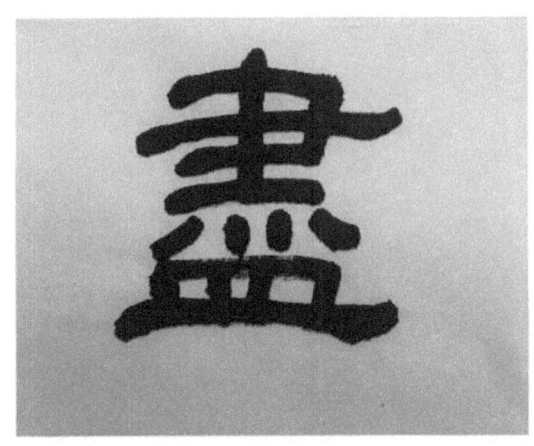

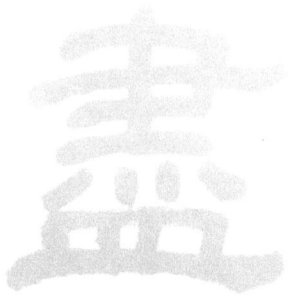

黄
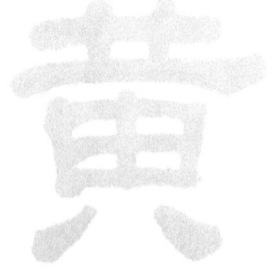

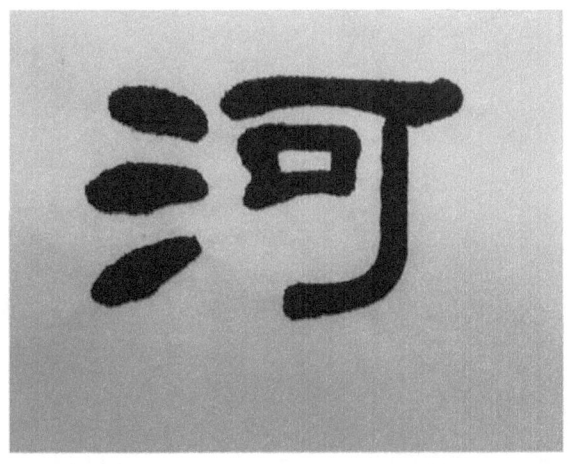

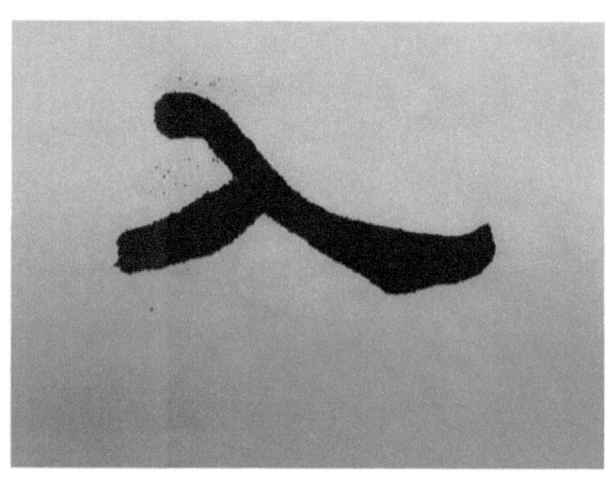

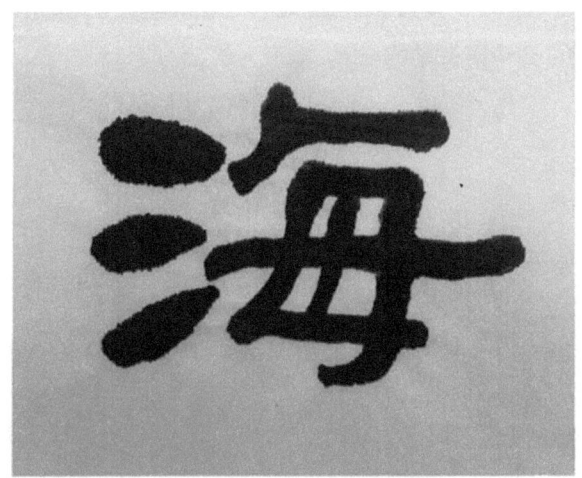

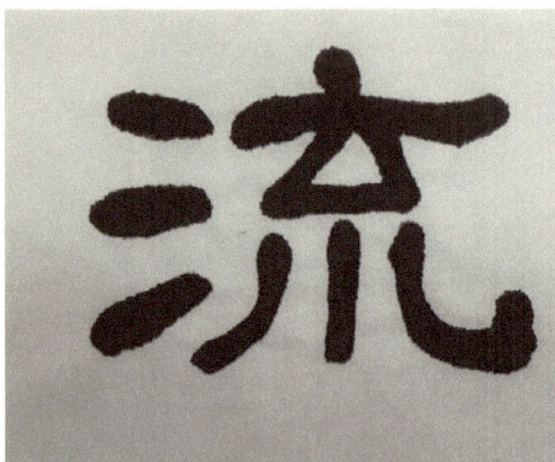

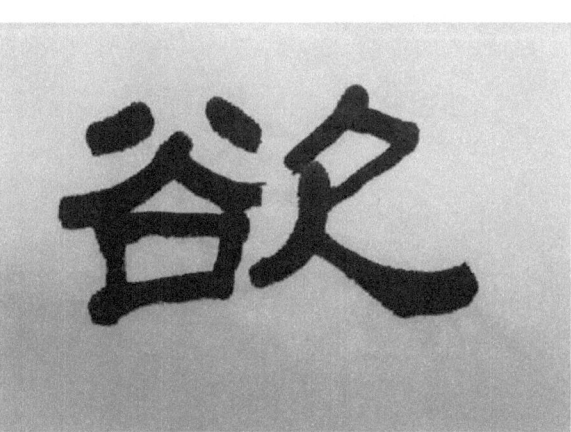

窮

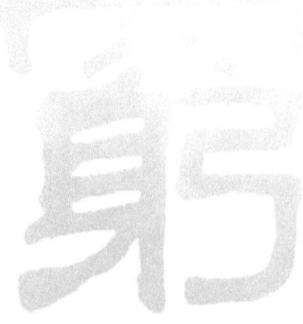

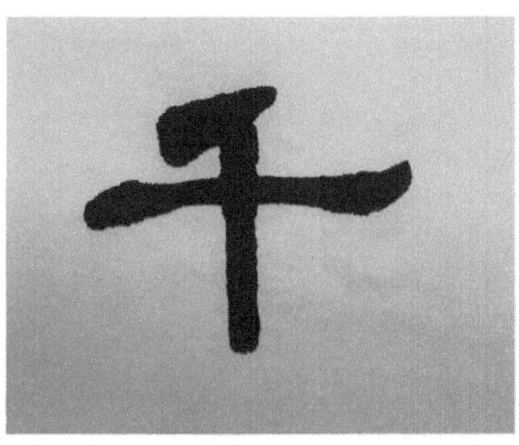

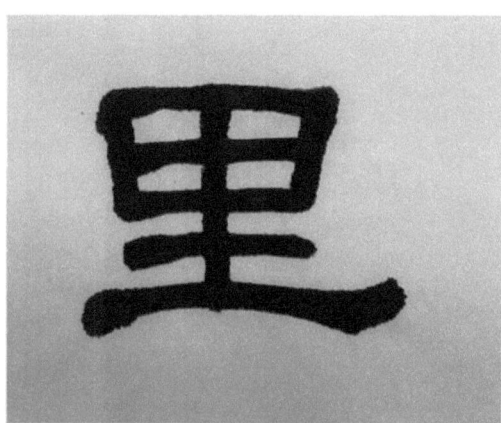

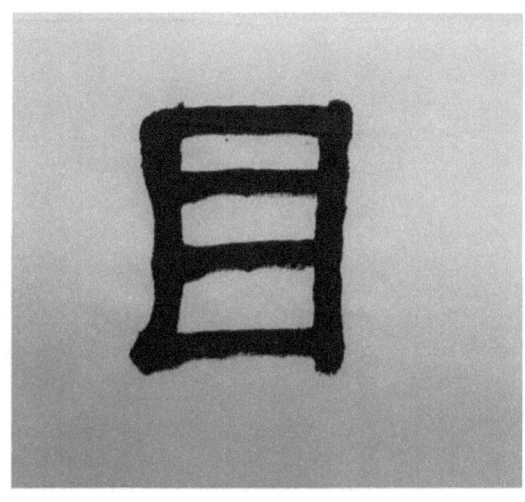

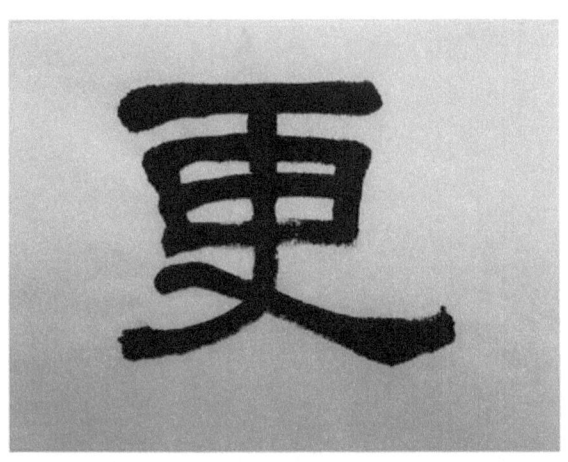

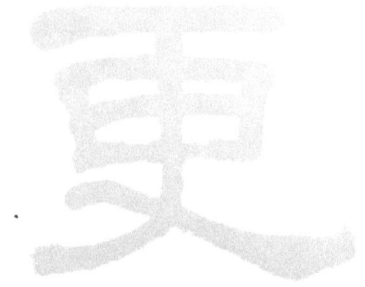

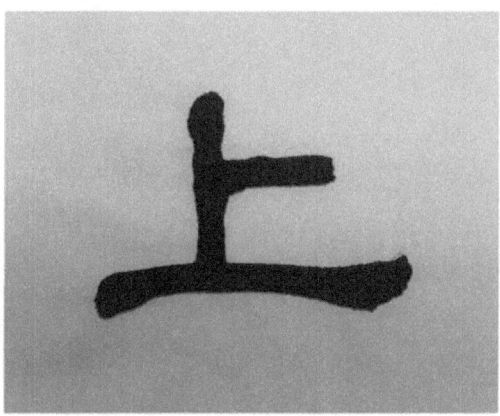

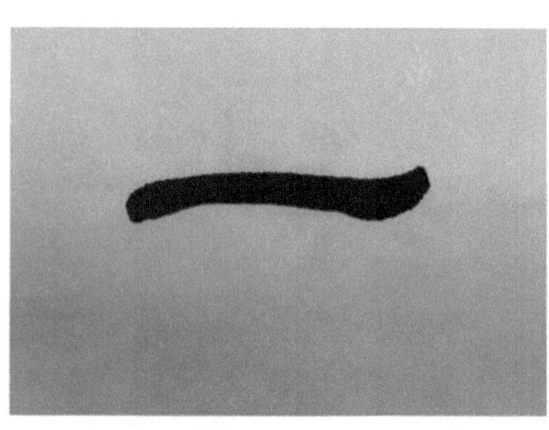

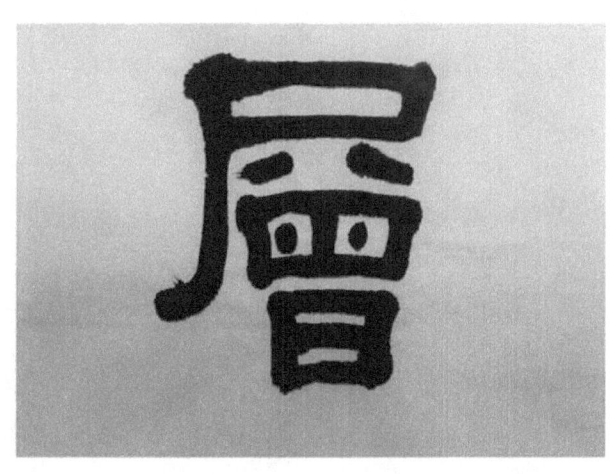

樓

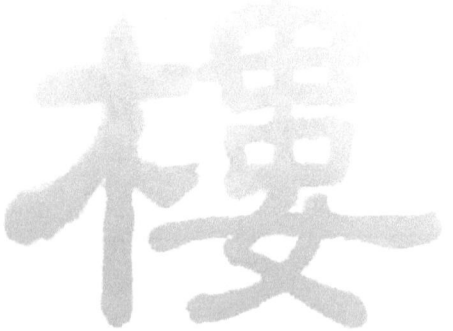

wonderful

www.ingramcontent.com/pod-product-compliance
Lightning Source LLC
Chambersburg PA
CBHW031522210526

45464CB00007B/3006